It's OK to Say No to Drugs

IT'S ALL UP TO YOU

By Susan Amerikaner
Illustrated by Fred Green

A WANDERER BOOK
Published by Simon & Schuster, Inc.

An RGA Creation. Copyright © 1986 by RGA Publishing Group, Inc. All rights reserved including the right of reproduction in whole or in part in any form. Published by WANDERER BOOKS a division of Simon & Schuster, Inc., Simon & Schuster Building, 1230 Avenue of the Americas, New York, New York 10020. WANDERER and colophon are registered trademarks of Simon & Schuster, Inc. IT'S OK TO SAY NO TO DRUGS is a trademark of RGA Publishing Group, Inc. Designed by Kathleen Westray. Manufactured in the United States of America.   10 9 8 7 6 5 4 3 2 1   ISBN: 0-671-62891-7

Take a look at those kids over there. What are they doing?

They're using drugs. And so are these kids.

They ask you to do drugs, too. You don't know what
to say. They ask you again. You've got to make a choice.
What should you do?

Say "NO!" It's OK to say "NO!" to drugs!

The kids keep asking you, but then they leave. You wonder
if you did the right thing.

After all, you want to fit in with the crowd. You don't want to stick out and look different.

You want to feel grown-up, and you don't want to be
called names, or made fun of. You think maybe you should
go after them....

Don't! It's normal to worry what people will think of you.
Everyone feels that way sometimes when they have to say
"NO!"

Think back to when Mom had to tell Mrs. Brown that she didn't have time to help with the school play. Mom didn't want anything to get in the way of their friendship, but she had to take a chance and say "NO!"

Then there was the time Dad felt awful because Uncle Phil asked him to go fishing and he couldn't. And remember the time your best friend wanted to go hiking when you had to babysit for your sister.

It can be hard to say "NO!", especially to friends, but there are times when you must. Doing what's right for you is the most important thing. Real friends understand that.

Drugs can make it tough for you to think, learn, walk, talk, and see. They can even make it hard for you to play.

If you take drugs you might even do things you'd be sorry for later.

Some kids may try to tell you that drugs will make you feel happy when you're feeling sad. But that is not a good way to deal with your feelings.

When you're unhappy, or angry, or scared, *talk about how you feel, instead.* Talk to someone who cares about you. How about the person who bought you this book?

Some kids may tell you that drugs are fun. But you already know many ways to have a good time.

Remember, it's your choice. You know what's best for you.
So...

say "NO!" It's OK to say "NO!" to drugs! In fact it's
much more than just OK: It's right, it's smart, it's safe, and ...

...it will make you feel GREAT!